Core-Self Discovery

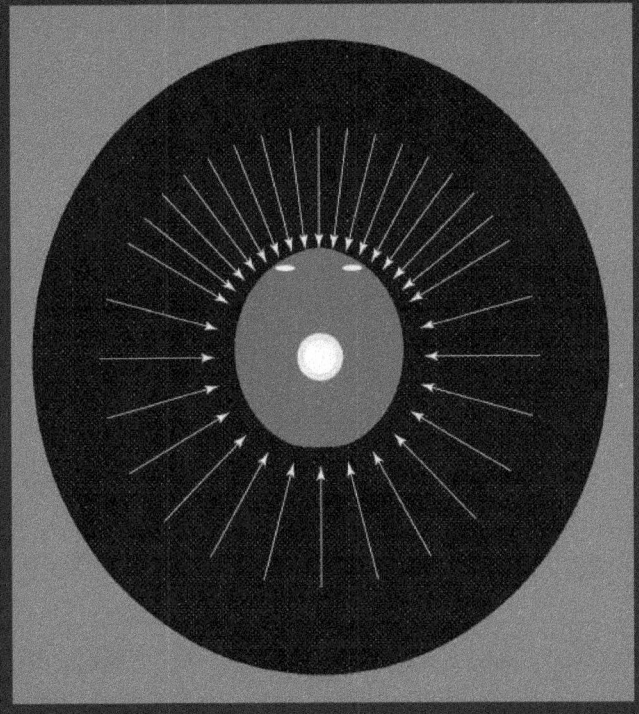

Michael Beloved ~ devaPriyā Yoginī

This publication is the text component of Core-Self Discovery course offered by inSelf Yoga©. This is adapted from Michael Beloved's *Meditation Pictorial* book. devaPriyā Yoginī (Erinn E. Tanner), who suggested this potential to the author, designed the format, composed text, and inspired diagrams which are not in *Meditation Pictorial*.

Graphics: Michael Beloved

Proofreaders: Marcia & Michael Beloved

Correspondence:

Michael Beloved
18311 NW 8th Street
Pembroke Pines
Florida 33029
USA

Email: axisnexus@gmail.com
devapriyayogini@gmail.com

Copyright © 2013 --- Michael Beloved / devaPriyā Yoginī

All rights reserved

Transmit / Reproduce / Quote with authors' **consent** only.

ISBN: 978-0-9884011-2-9

LCCN: 2013909563

Table of Contents

Introduction 4

Diagrams ~ Instructions 7

Index 62

Series 64

    Commentaries 64

    Explained Series 68

    Meditation Series 70

    Specialty Topics 71

    English Series 74

Authors 78

Introduction

The views of the picture-maps are as if looking through the skull.

If you find any diagrams difficult, proceed with those you grasp. Practice the difficult ones separately in different sessions.

Eyes should be closed during the meditation, except when viewing a diagram.

For beginners, a noise free, dark or dimly lit place is preferable. A room or closet with ample ventilation is ideal.

The initial steps of the procedure help the meditator become directly aware of the presence of subtle energy contained in the head. Becoming familiar with the subtle energy, and how it can be directed by the personal will, is important as we learn how to take control of the mind.

The alternative is to ignore the components of the mind, disregard the possibility of refining the power of the will, and continue living our lives being pushed and pulled about by an energy system which is too subtle to perceive. This energy system was present at the onset of the universe. It existed before I became conscious of myself as a human being. I was mostly unaware of it. I incorrectly identified the combination consciousness as myself, feeling that I am my body and its senses, that I am my mind and that I must comply with the impulsive energies

Yogis observe and investigate this psychological interaction with physical reality. They use refinement of the will to assert control in order to play a part in how the body apparatus manages the individual life experience. The yogi's objective is ambitious. It is an escape by transcending the matrix of ever-expanding social involvement which sets the stage for repeated birth and death.

The yogi (yogini) adopts new habits, abandons undesirable ones and disciplines himself (herself) through meditation to elevate the vibration of the subtle body in order to ascend to higher planes. The serious meditator knows that the alternative is to remain enclosed in this current vibrational mode for continued incarnations in which we can expect more of the same traumatic condition. Trauma, as Buddha explained, is the nature of this existence.

We review our fragile physical circumstance. We look at our present condition and the history of the earth. We are honest with ourselves about the intrinsic nature of ever-changing matter.

We act for the reduction of trauma.

Spiritual liberation is one of the results of a successful meditation practice.

This procedure should result in discovery of the core-self with increased control of the subtle energies in the head.

Diagrams ~ Instructions

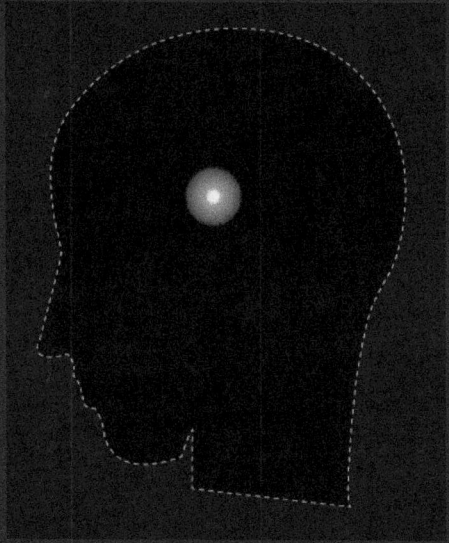

The core-self's default location is at the energy convergence-center of the subtle head.

In Sanskrit this core-self is addressed as the ātma. This means the individual particle self. Its location has an aura of spiritual potency. It is centrally situated in the psychological energy of the subtle head.

Resolving to use the power of personal will, our intention is to practice moving energy throughout the head space in one direction, then another and at various angles. We will project from the center, and then retract the focus into the same central place.

Subtle energy in the head is active. It is dynamic. It sponsors the functions of mind. If an individual has no or very little control of this essential energy, nature will use it impulsively. This may produce habits which further dis-empower the core-self.

Putting will power to work in moving this energy will aid us in assuming control over the orientation and location of its use, aiding in our efforts toward meditation.

This practice refines our use of personal will. It gives the opportunity to influence subtle energy and to cause insight-awareness of the spiritual self.

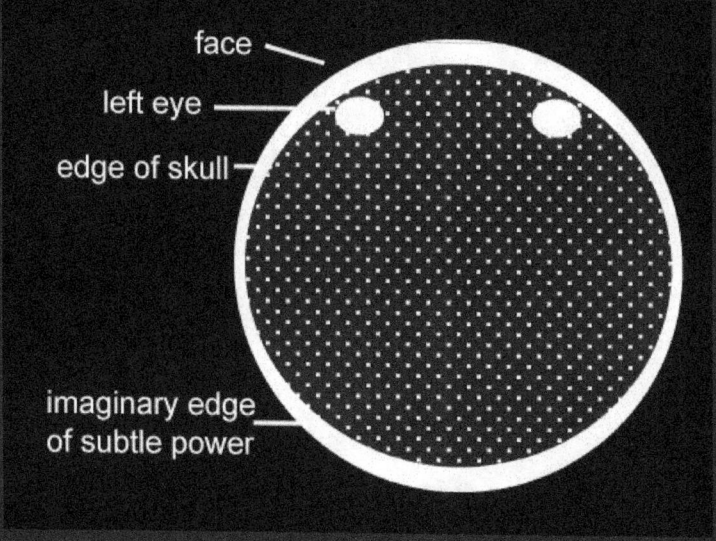

Contain all feelings, thoughts, and ideas, within the skull.

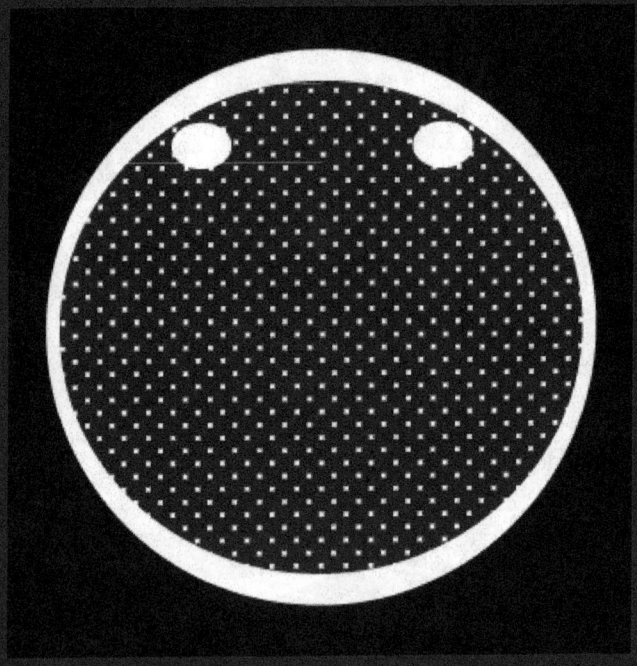

Ignore any activity outside the skull.

Observe the speckled darkness inside your head.

It is all around spherically but usually noticed in the front only, due to focus orientation through the face of the head.

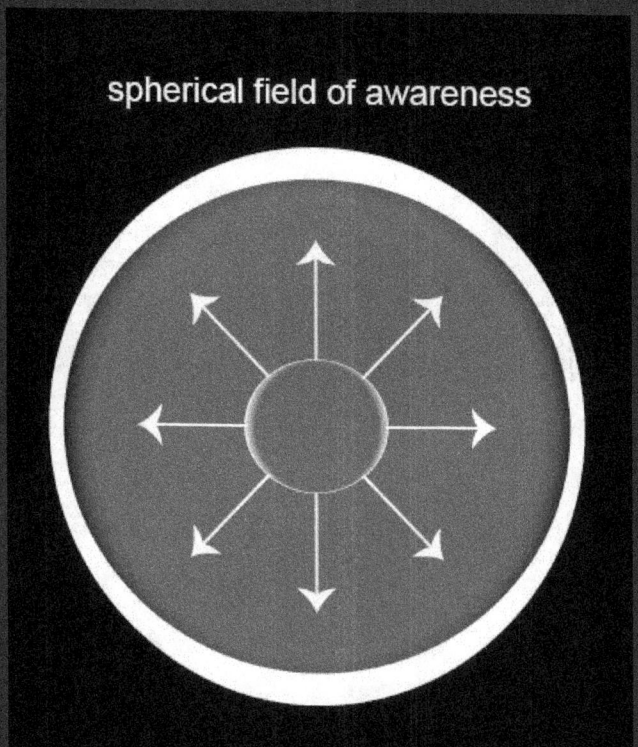

With the eyes closed and awareness contained within the mind space notice 360 degree awareness perception.

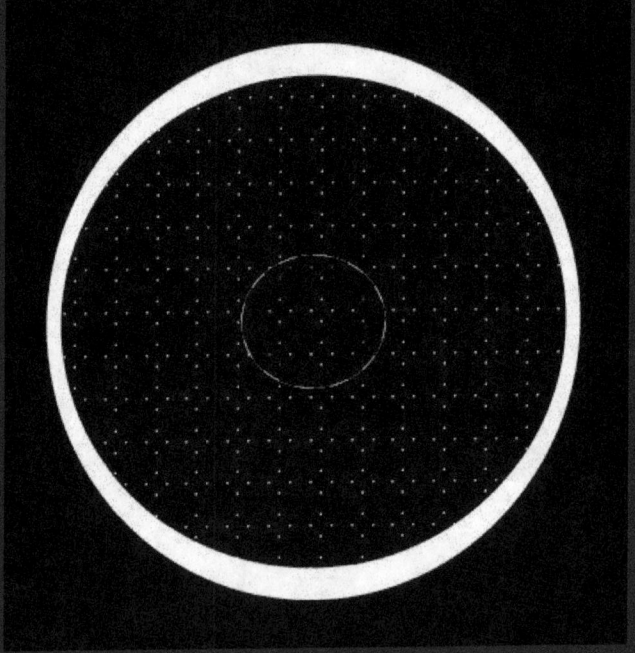

Examine the back, sides and front of the mind space. You are no longer limited to forward facing awareness.

Continue to withdraw interest in anything outside the skull.

Ask yourself: Where am I?

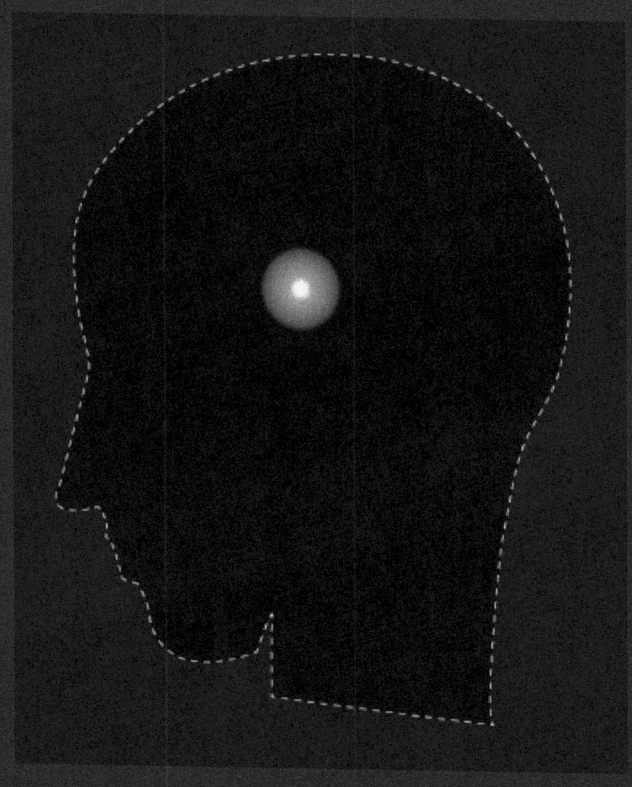

Locate the sense of *"I am"* in a radiant energy in the center of the head.

Bring awareness to the eyes.

Diagrams~Instructions

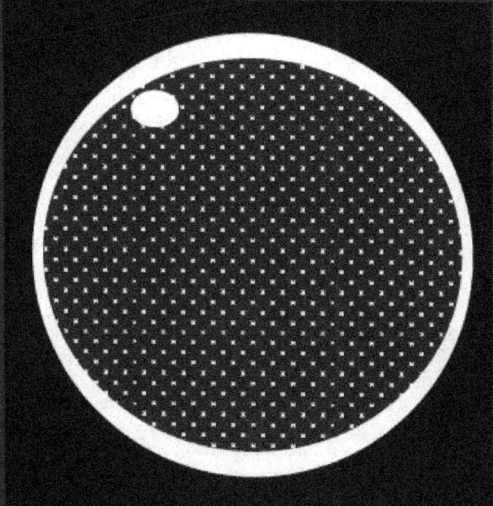

Focus on the left eyeball.

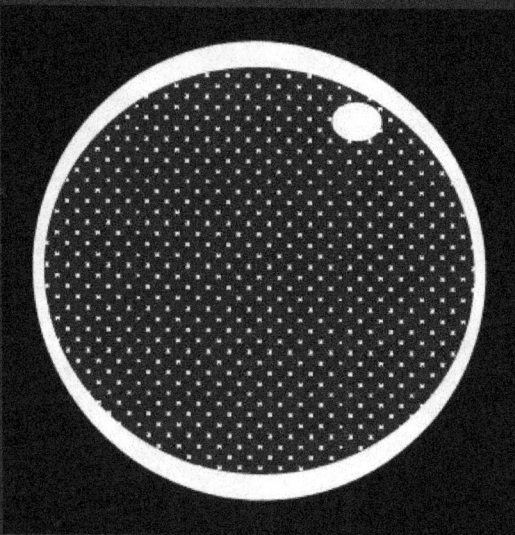

Switch focus to the right eyeball.

Be aware of both eyeballs as spaces of subtle power.

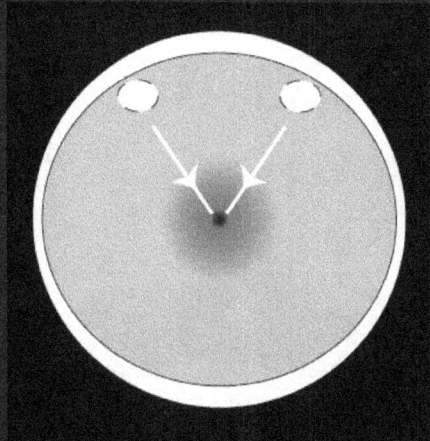

Trace the energy of both eyeballs back to the common point where the optic power originates. To do this, mentally retract the eyeballs.

Then push them out.

That identifies the focusing energy.

Direct the energy backwards from both eyes. Follow the trail of energy to the origin of optic power at the center of head.

Contract the eyeballs tightly. Focus into the eyeballs.

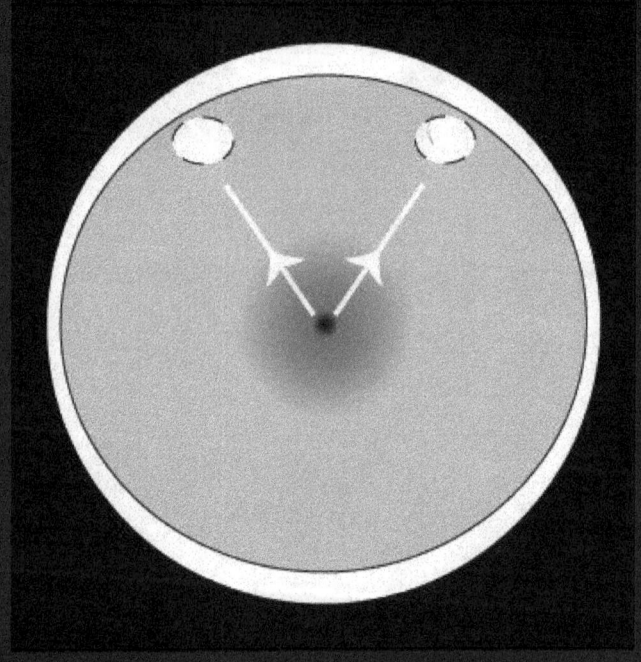

Send energy into the eyeballs.

Diagrams~Instructions

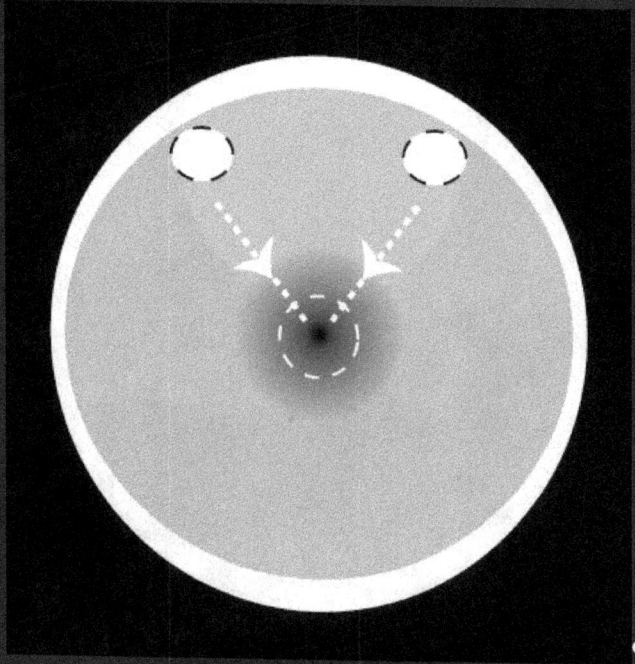

Relax eyelids, soften eyeballs.

Become aware of the contained mental power surrounding the optic meeting point.

(*Dotted lines in diagram indicate partial drainage of soul power.)

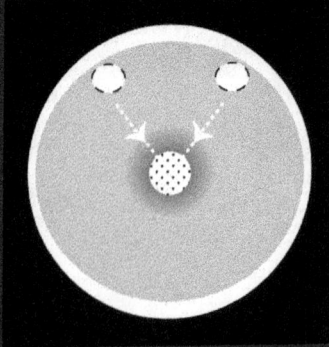

Pull energy from eyeballs back into the central head by will power.

In the effort to do this, physical muscles may react to mimic the mental action. Repeatedly do this and practice for some time until the mental action operates without physical response.

This practice causes a separation between the physical and psychological aspects of the self.

Intentionally retract the optic power. Focus on intense soul power.

Repeatedly do this. Then relax the eyeballs.

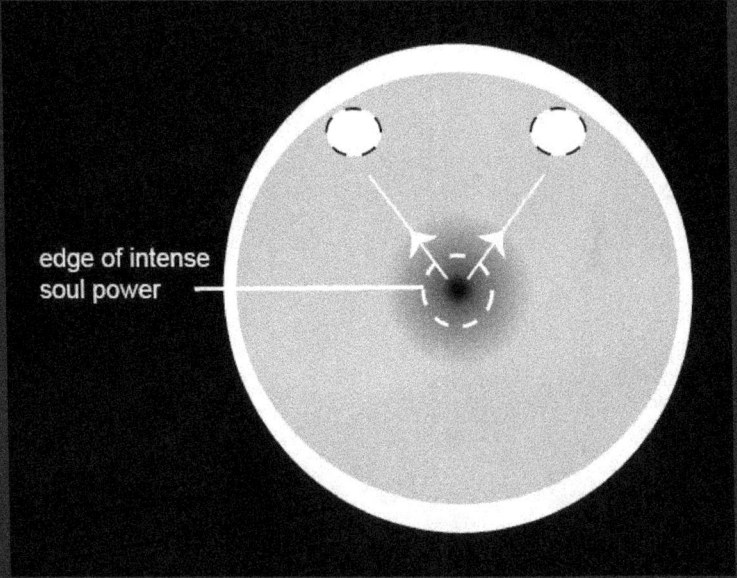

Push subtle eyeballs outward by will power only.

Assert mental power through the optic channels to the eyeballs.

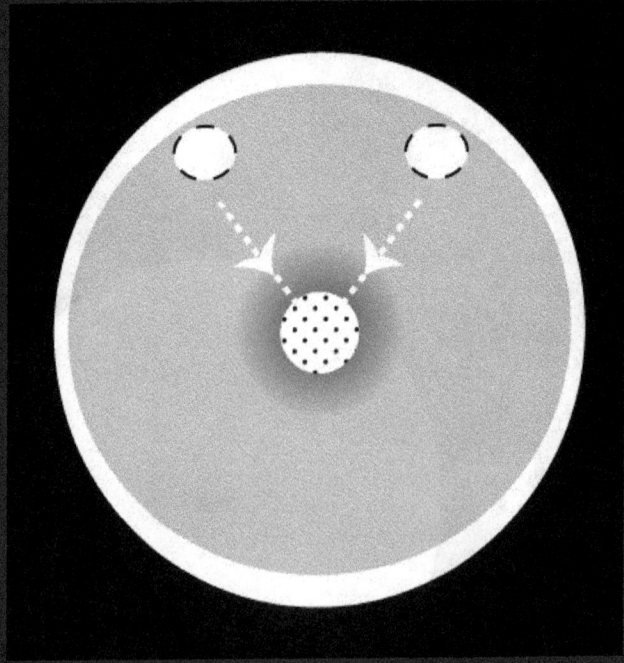

Draw the energy back into the optic meeting point in the center of consciousness:

- Question yourself:
- Where am I?

Does this energy have a core or center?

Diagrams~Instructions

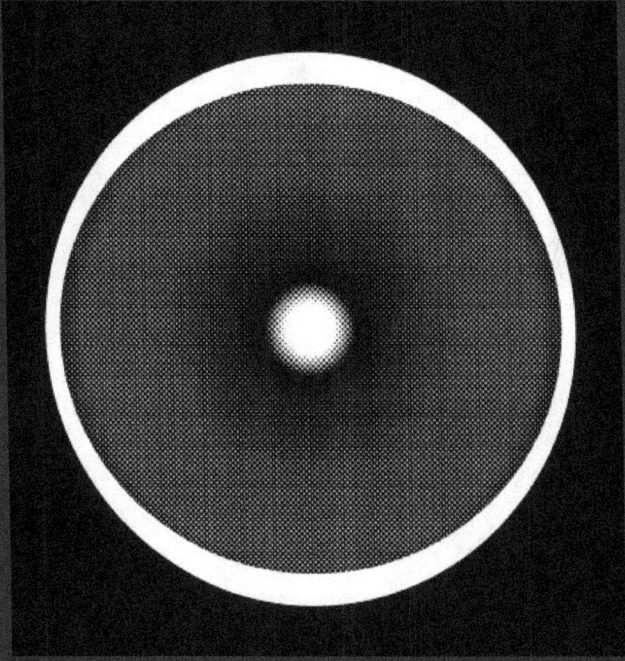

Focus fully on this central radiant energy.

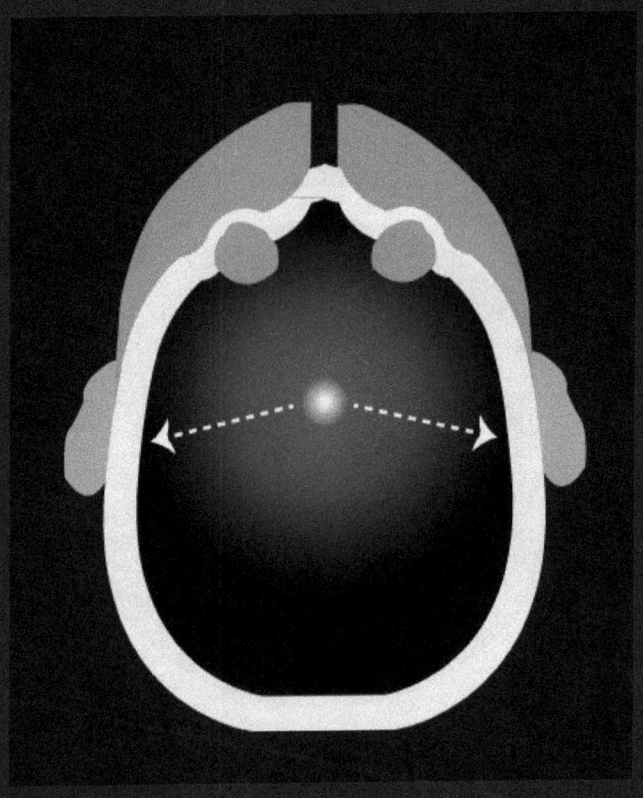

Use will power to move central energy sideways, outward through the ears.

Feel subtle energy moving through the ears from the center of the head.

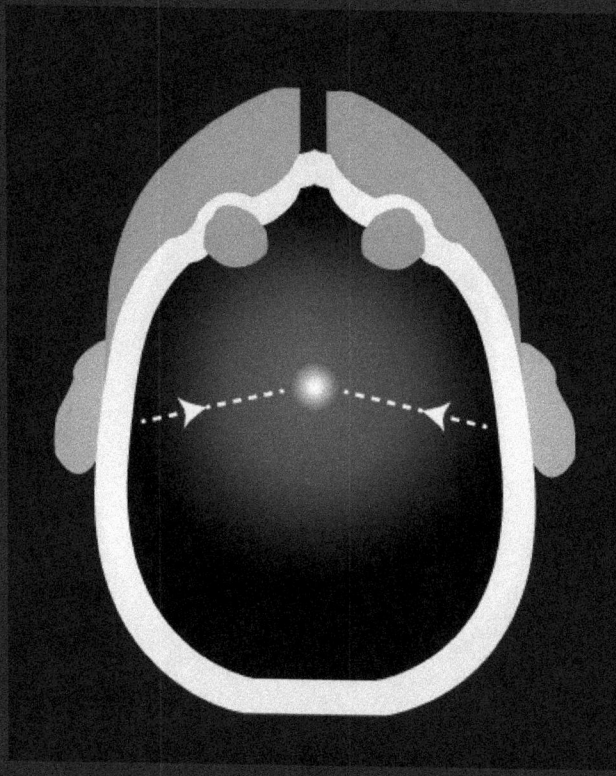

Pull subtle energy back in through the ears, into the center of the head.

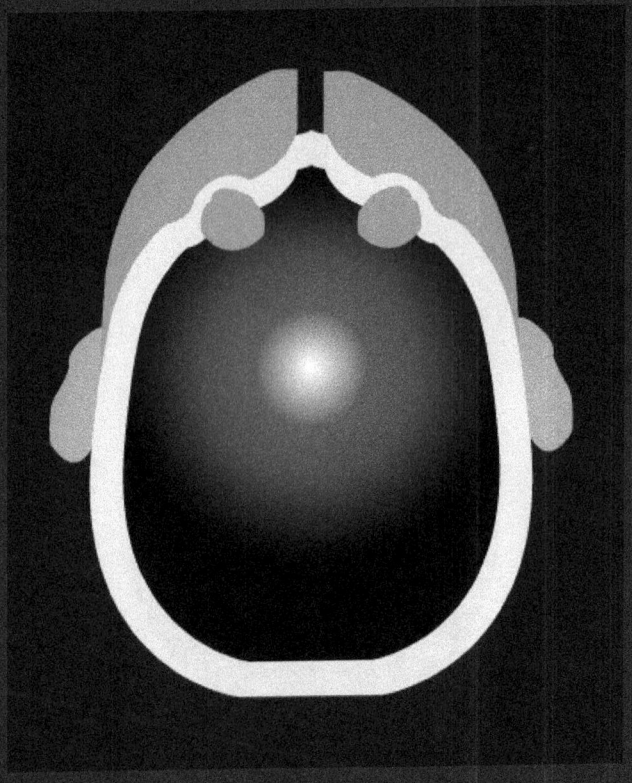

Be aware of the radiant center.

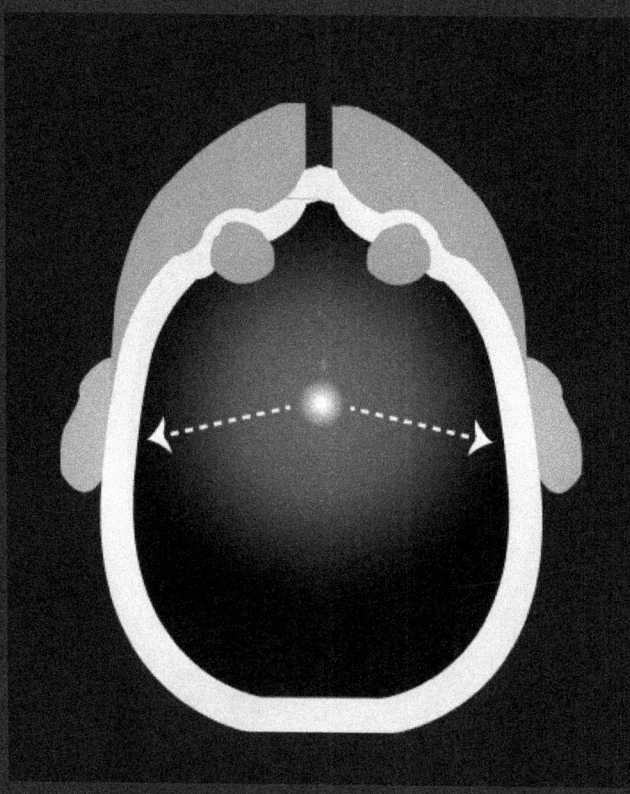

Again, move the energy from the center, out the sides of the head, through the ears.

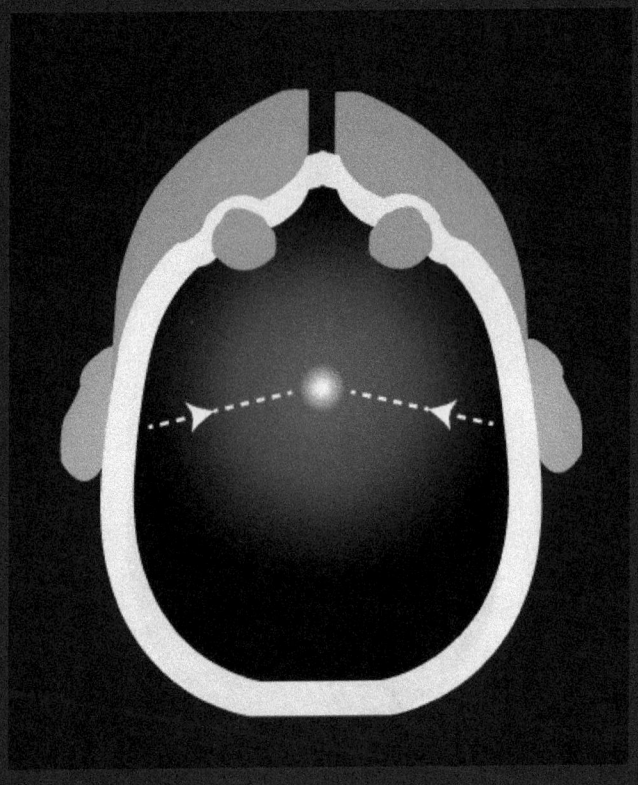

Retract the energy back in to the center of the skull space.

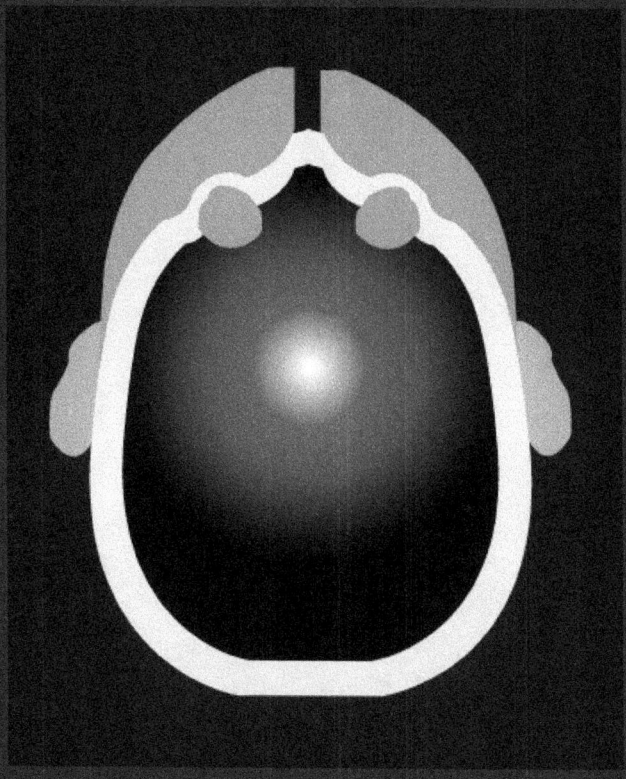

Be aware of the energetic center of the head.

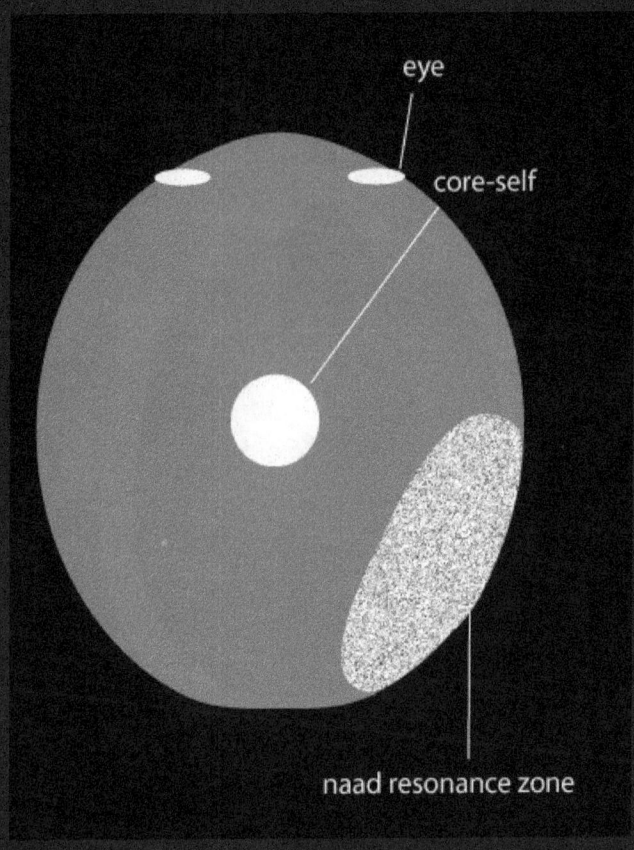

Notice if you hear or sense a sound current in the ears or head space.

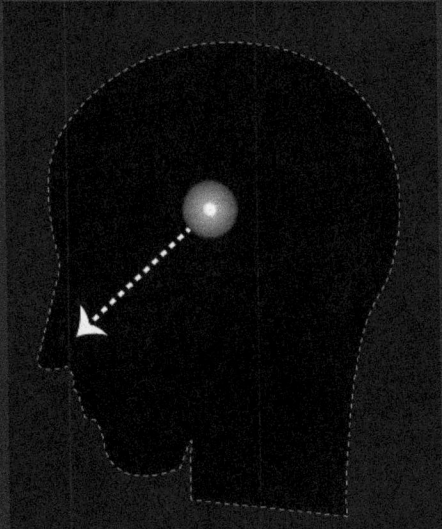

Increase the duration of breath.

Do a longer inhale and longer exhale.

From the radiant center, project subtle energy downward through both nostrils.

Project this energy during the longer exhale.

As breath passes out mentally move energy with the air.

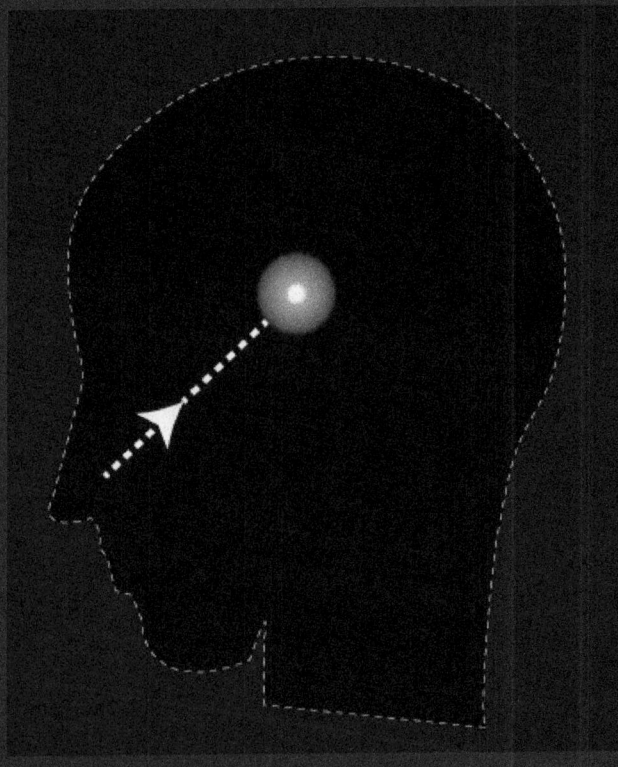

During the inhale, as breath is drawn in, pull, fresh subtle energy upward into the center of head.

Repeat this until you feel surcharged.

On the last breath in, keep the energy at the core of consciousness, while resuming the normal breathing rate.

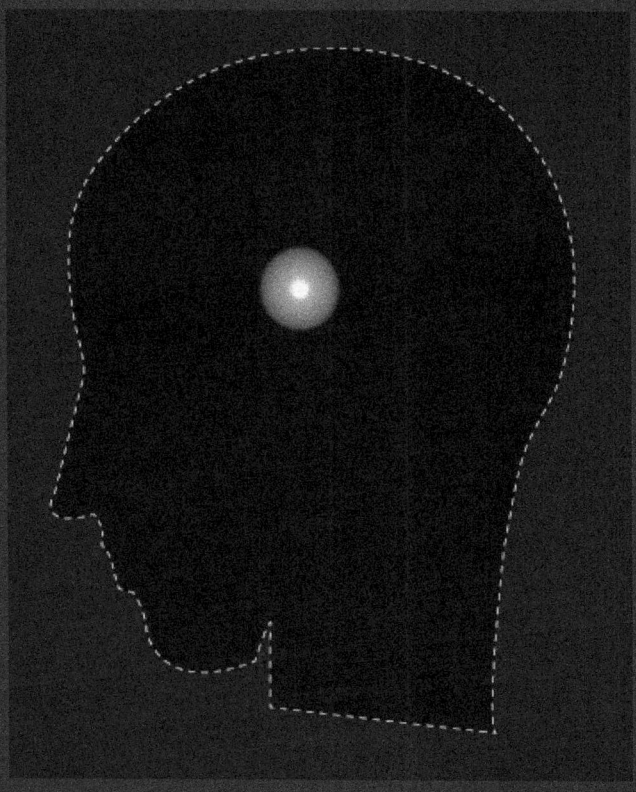

Be aware of the radiant energy in the center of head.

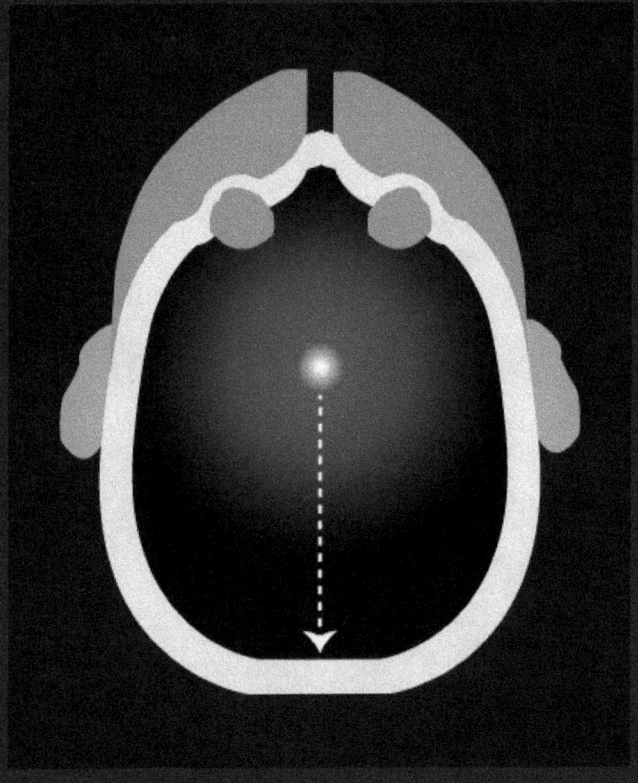

From the center, using will power, send energy straight through the back of the skull.

Energy will flow outward through the very back of the head, removing dullness and tensions from this area.

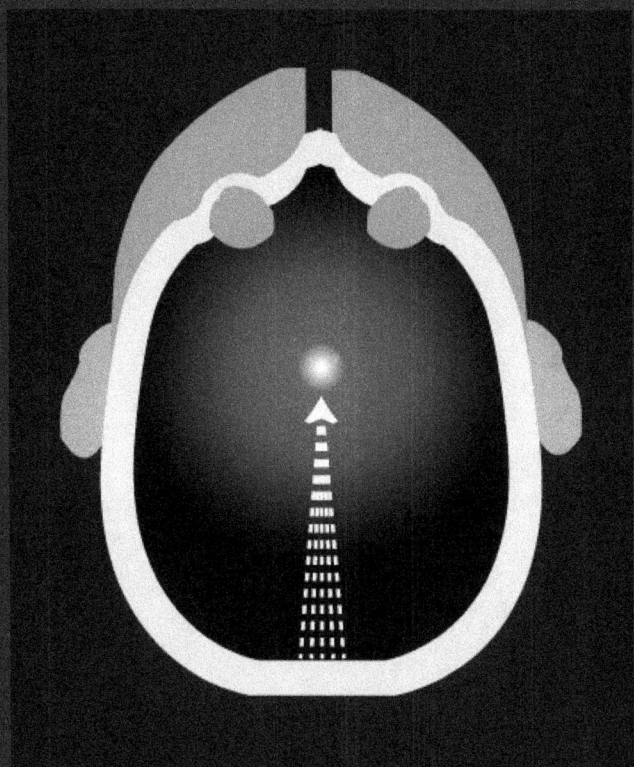

Willfully bring fresh clean energy in through the back of skull, into the center.

Please repeat this practice until it becomes spontaneous.

Notice the reservoir of energy in the middle of the head.

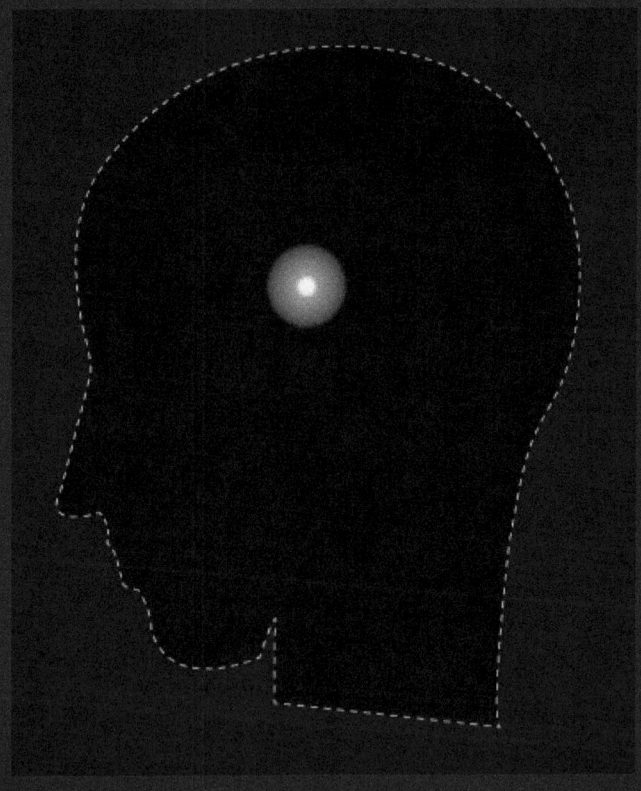

Ask yourself, *Where am I?*

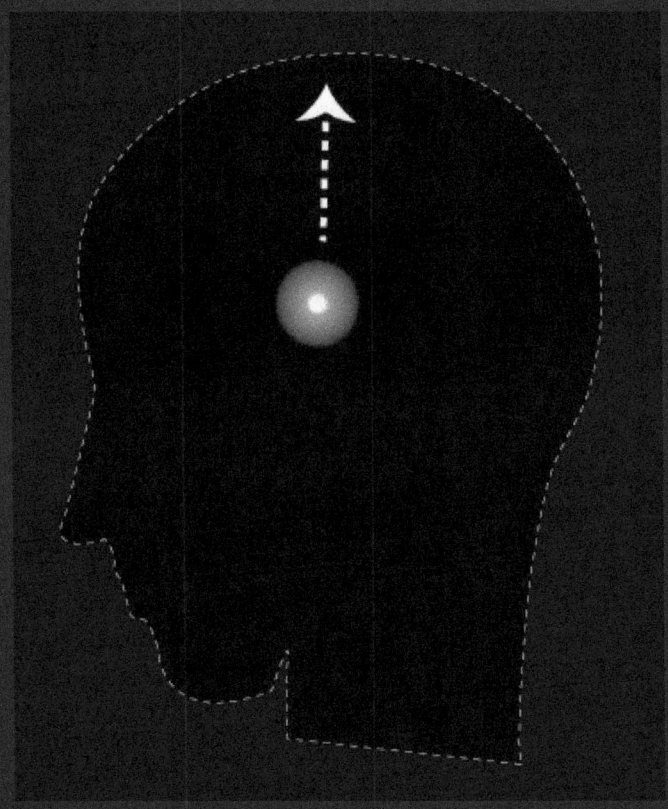

From the radiant center send energy through the top of the head, straight upward.

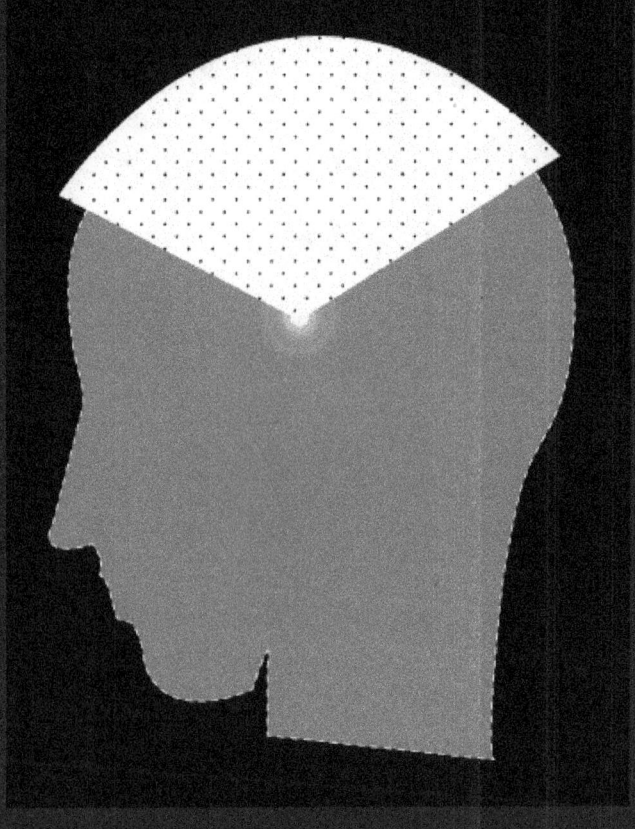

With focus and determination, draw clean energy downward through the top of head, bringing it into the magnetic center of head.

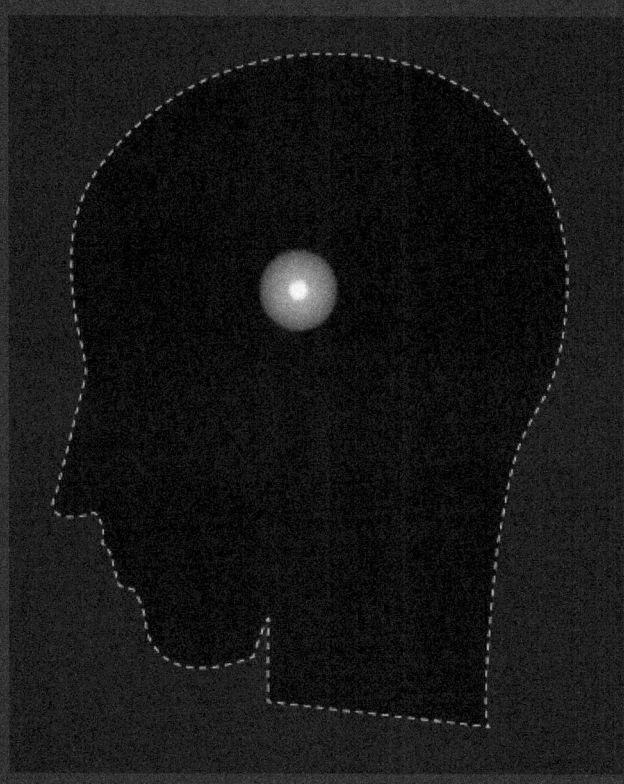

Examine the quality of the energy in the head center.

Remain focused on the radiant effulgence for some time.

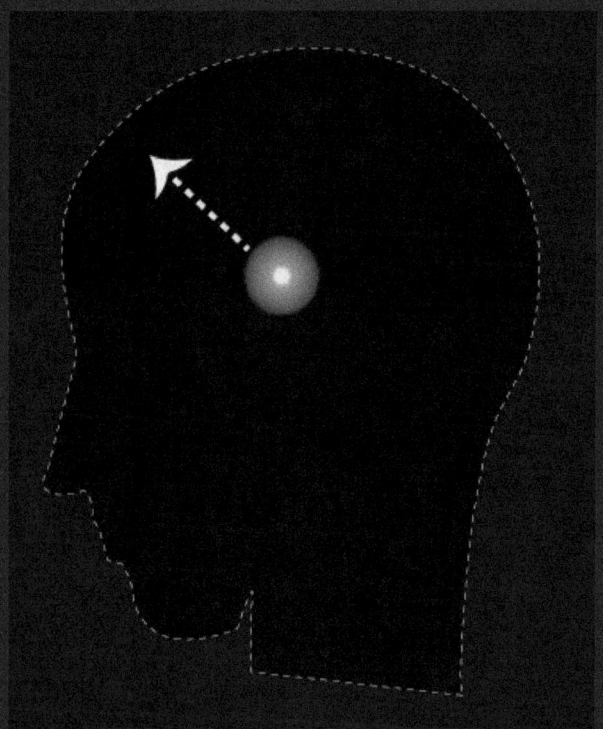

Using will power, push energy from the head center upward through the upper part of forehead. Project the energy in an upward angle through the expanse of the forehead.

Shatter and dissipate tensions or dullness from this area while pushing energy through.

Diagrams~Instructions 41

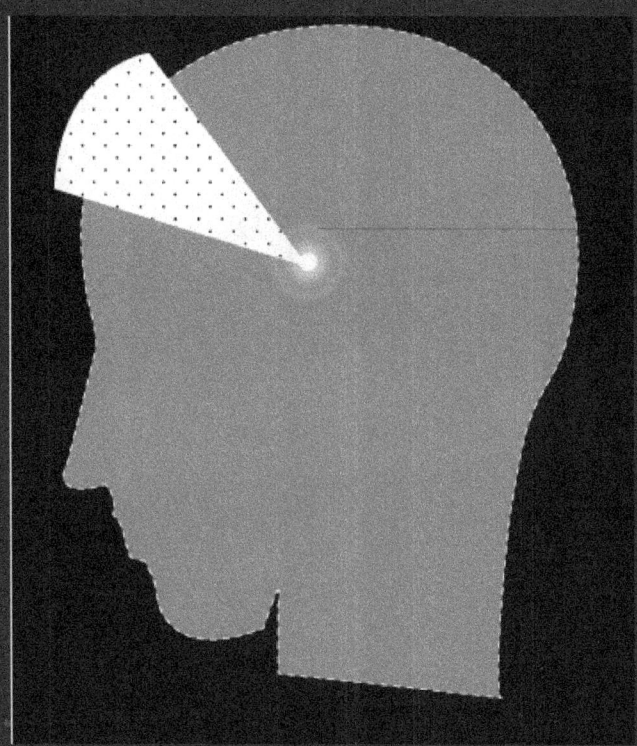

Bring clean energy back in through the same forehead space, into the center of the skull.

Repeat this practice to integrate it.

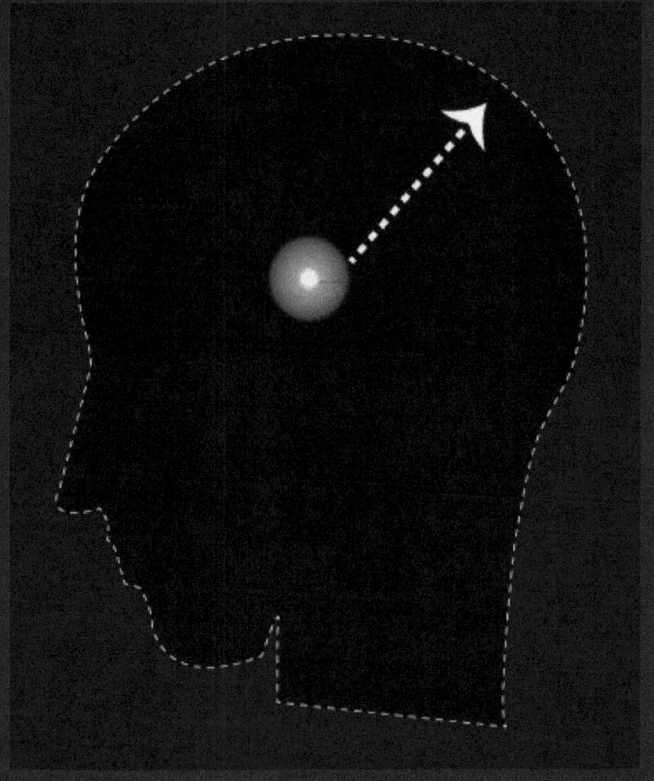

At the angle shown above, project energy from the radiant center through the back of the upper skull.

Shatter and release tensions from this area.

Move energy through the expanse of the upper back portion of skull.

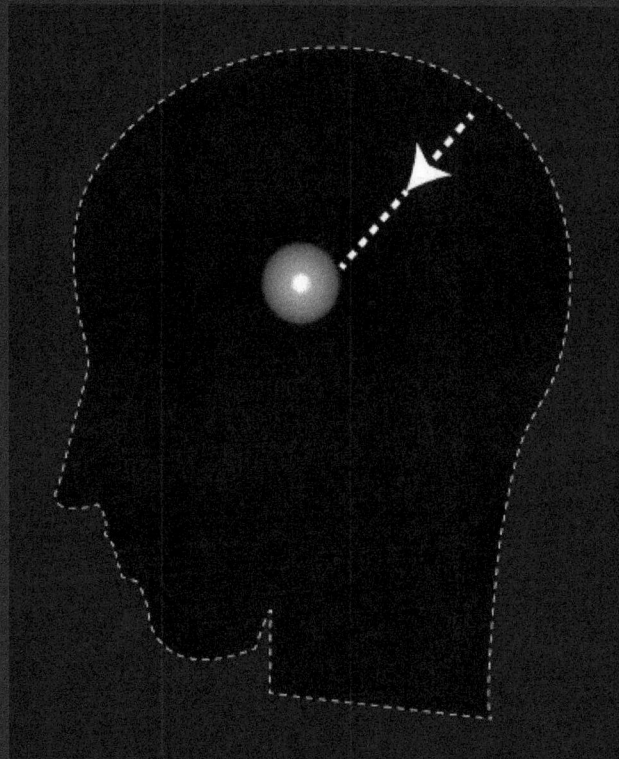

With determination bring fresh energy in through the same location.

Let clean fresh energy flow into the existential central head space.

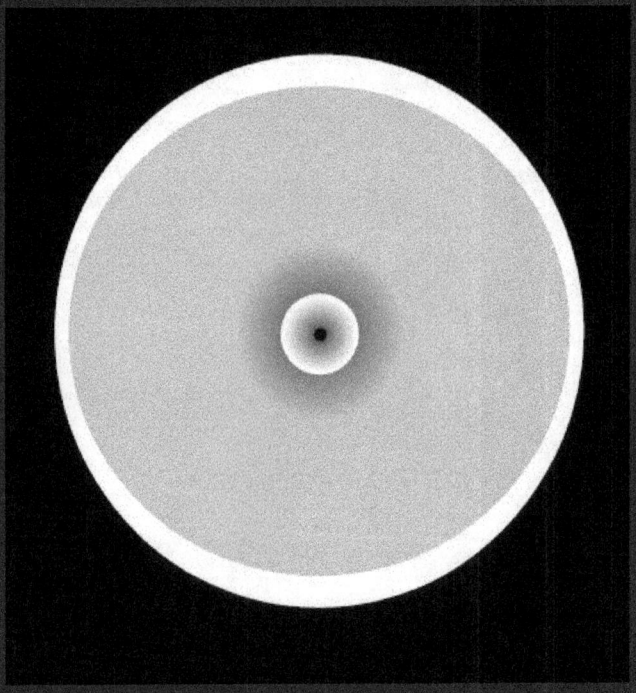

Remain aware in the center of the head.

Relax all energy in the head. Remain there for some time.

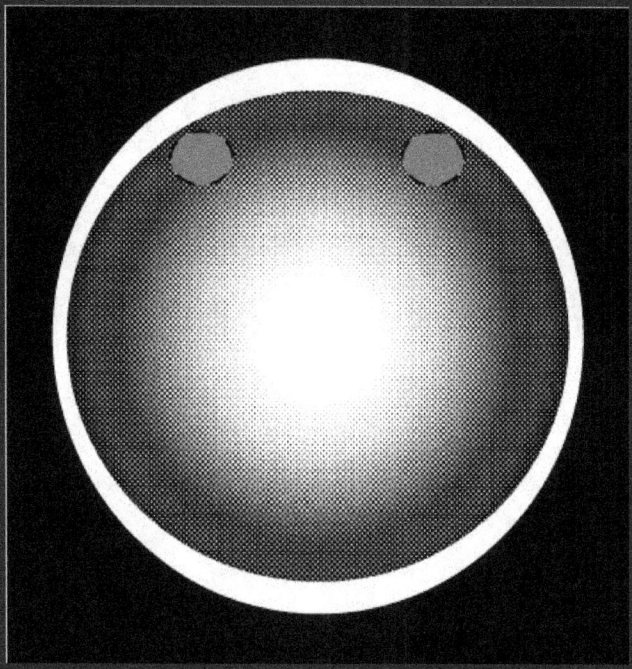

Feel consciousness spreading through the skull space.

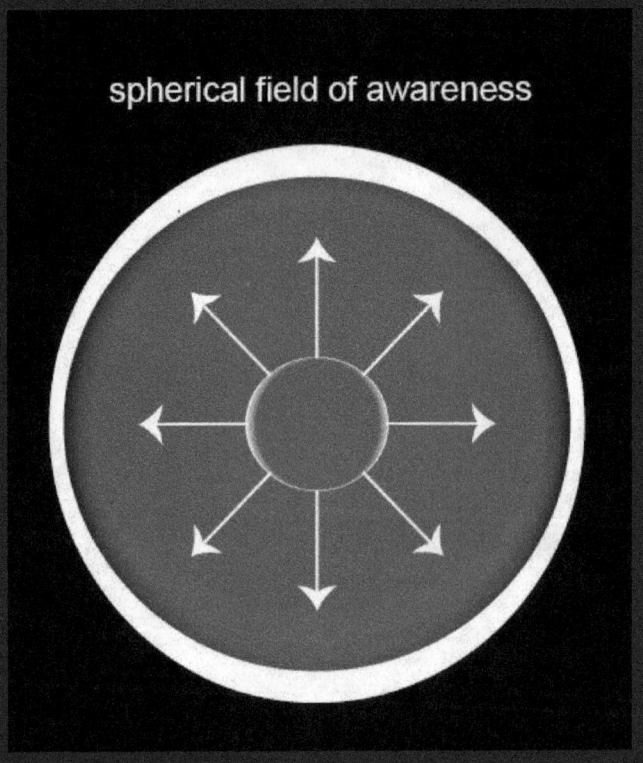

Feel soul power expanding outward in all directions.

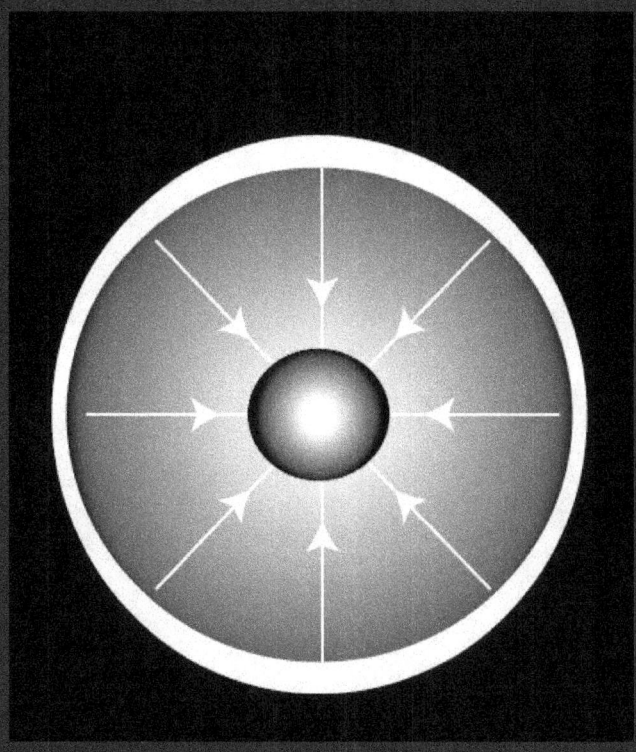

Reverse the expansion by mentally retracting the energy of consciousness in all directions. Direct it to the intense radiant awareness in the center.

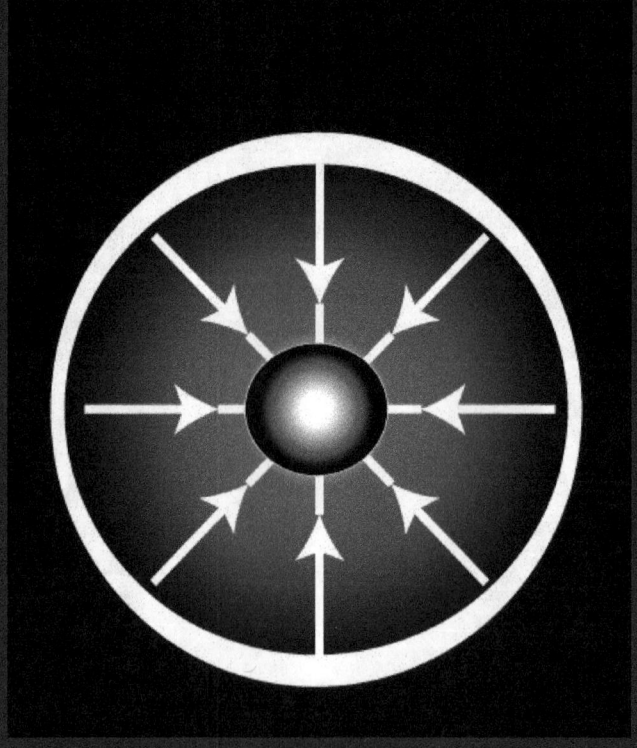

Detect the limits of intense consciousness

Retract consciousness inwards with a stronger pulling focus.

Shrink and intensify the consciousness.

Concentrate it.

Remain in this state for some time.

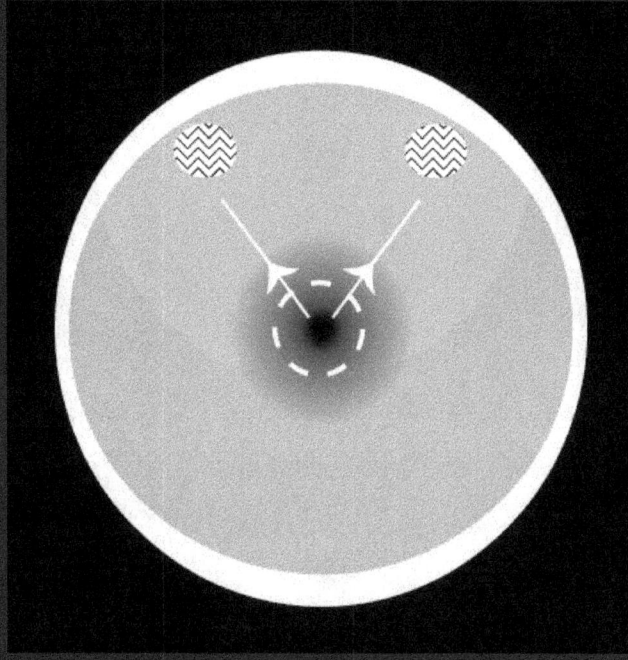

Re-assert optic power by sending energy to the eyeballs. Stay aware of the origin point of the optic channels.

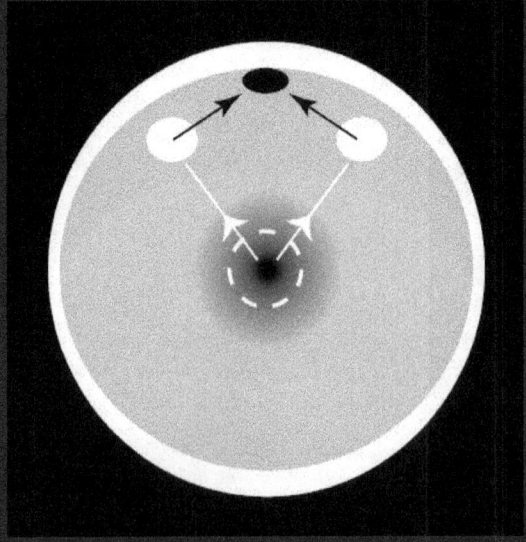

With eyes closed focus through the eyeballs to the dark space between the eyebrows. Focus on that dark space.

Feel the energy moving through the subtle circuitry from the optic meeting point through the eyeballs to the space between the eyebrows.

If the focus becomes stalled in the eyeballs, make repeated attempts to move it to the dark space between the eyebrows.

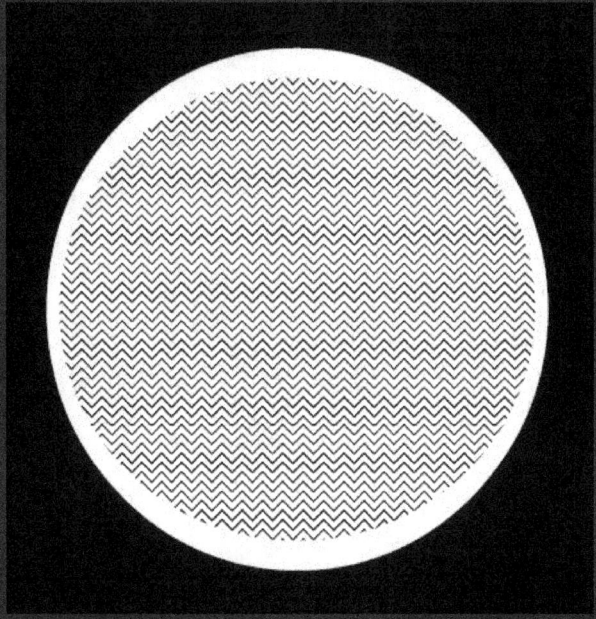

Stop the release of energy originating at the optic meeting point. Enter a state of no focus throughout the head space.

In the state of no-focus, make efforts to determine where you are.

Try to locate the I-self in that abstract space of consciousness.

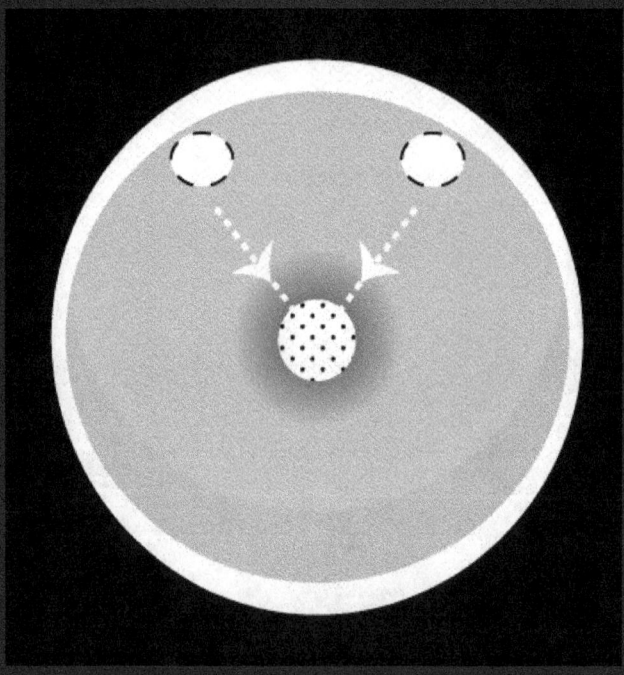

Locate the eyeballs and trace backwards to the meeting point of the optic force.

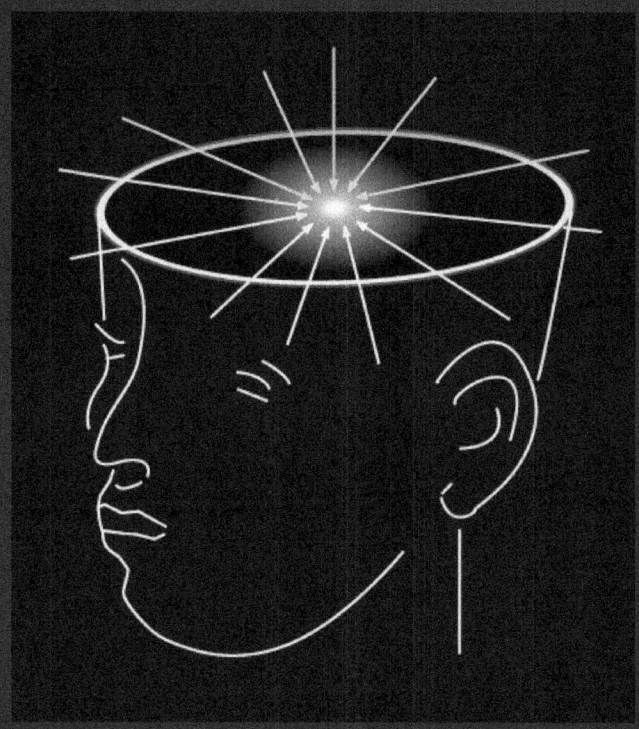

Retract the energy of consciousness from all directions inward.

Direct it to the intense radiant awareness in the center.

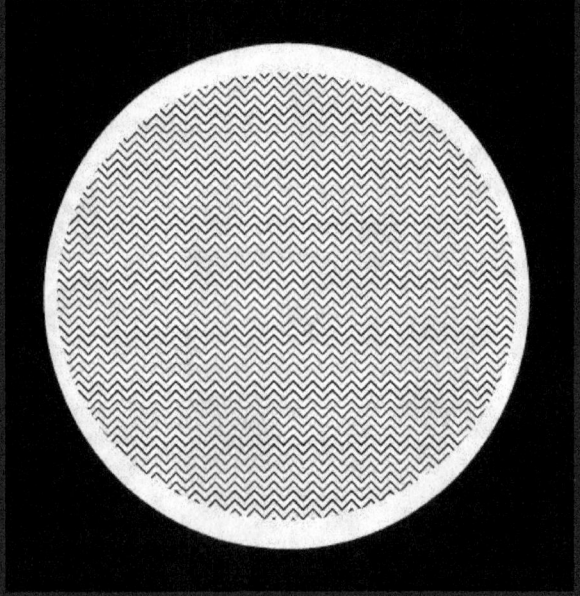

Diffuse the central consciousness.

Allow the central consciousness to expand.

Reflect on the vagueness of the mental space.

Consider how memories, reasoning ability, emotions, feelings, random imaginations and day dreaming ceased.

How do these mental constructions occur?

Can this process be visualized in detail?

Diffuse the subtle power

Allow the subtle power to expand

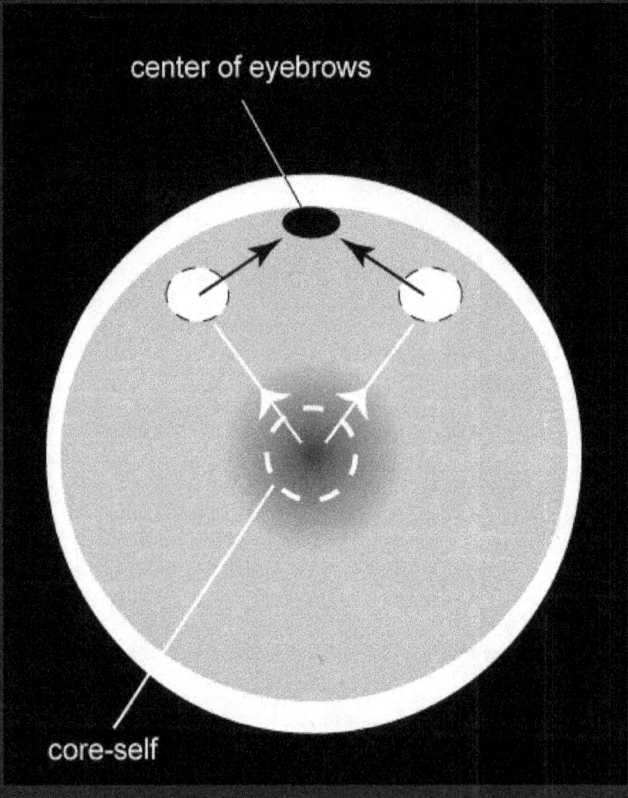

Refocus optic channel to the darkness at center of eyebrows.

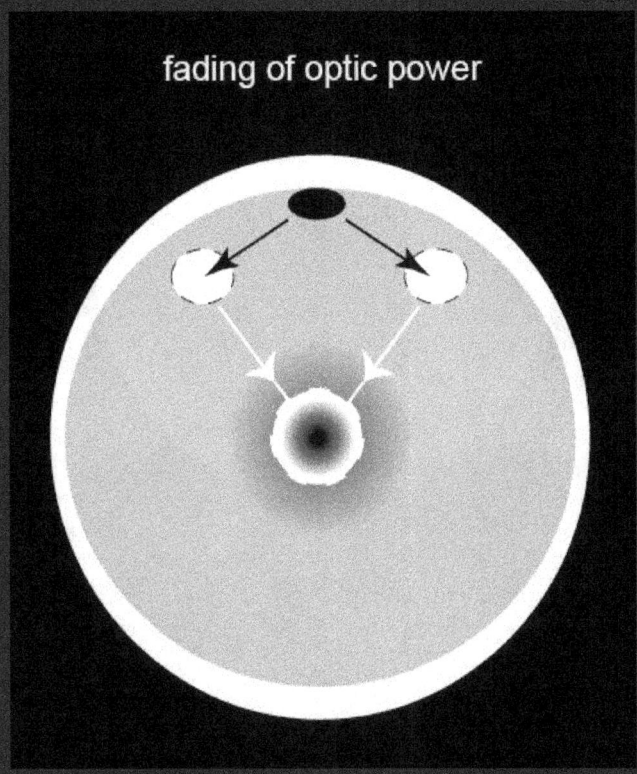

Gently and willfully withdraw the energy from the optic channels and return it to the origin point.

Slowly relax the focus.

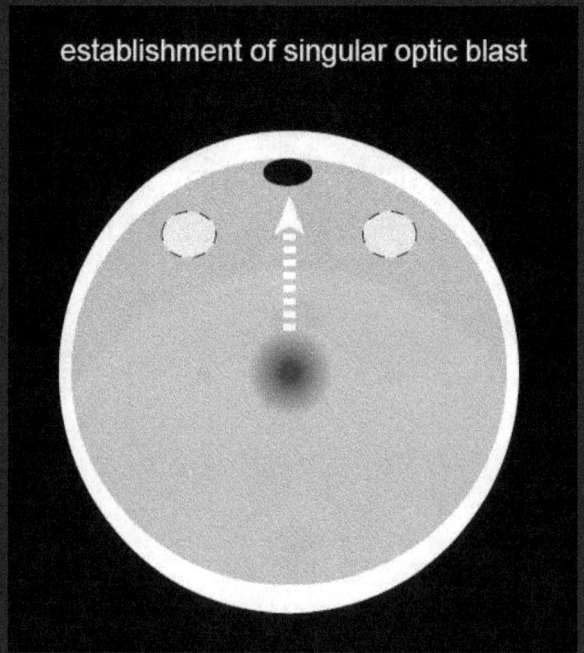

Establish a singular blast by sending energy directly from the optic meeting point to the darkness between the eyebrows.

The dark space between the eyebrows is the location of a subtle or third eye.

Keep energy projecting through that area.

Feel as if the optic center is blasting a flow of energy through the center of the eyebrows.

Diagrams~Instructions

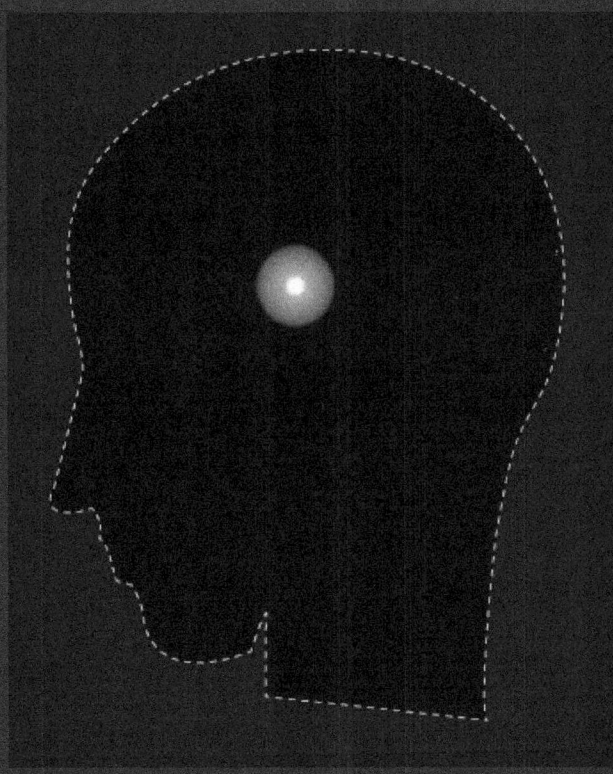

Relax and return focus to the radiant core-self at the center of head.

These practices should result in a deeper awareness of the core-self.

These enhance psychic perception.

This will strengthen willpower and increase the degree of psychological control.

Do this repeatedly until you master these procedures.

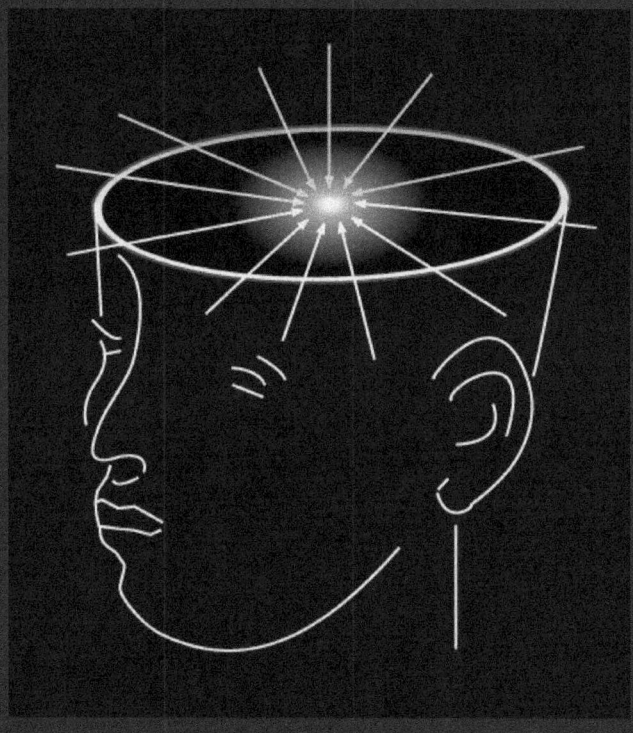

Index

A, B, C
abstract space, 51
ātma, 7
aura of spiritual potency, 7
awareness, 360 degree, 11
awareness, insight, 8
back of skull, 34
birth and death, 4
Buddha, 6
center of consciousness, 22
closet, 4
components, mind, 4
constructions, 54
contained power, 19
convergence-center, 7
core or center, 22
core-self's location, 7
current, sound, 30

D, E, F, G, H
day dreaming, 54
default location, 7
degree, 11
diffuse power, 55
dreaming, 54
ears, 24
emotions, 54
energetic center, 29
existential central, 43
eyeballs, subtle, 16
feelings, 9, 54
forward awareness, 12

I, J, K
I am, 13
I am my body, 4
ideas, 9
imagination, 54
impulsive energies, 4
incarnations, 6
individual particle, 7
insight-awareness, 8
intense radial awareness, 47, 53
I-self, 51

L, M, N, O
liberation, 6
limits of intense
    consciousness, 48
location, core-self's, 7
matrix, 4
memories, 54
mental constructions, 54
no-focus, 51
onset of the universe, 4
optic point, 19, 58
optic originates, 17

P, Q. R
particle, 7
perception, 11
picture-maps, 4
radial awareness, 47
radiant core-self, 59
random imaginations, 54
reasoning ability, 54
reduction of trauma, 6
reservoir of energy, 36
room, 4

S, T, U, V, W, X, Y, Z
Sanskrit, 7
singular blast, 58
soul power, 46
sound current, 30
spiritual liberation, 6
spiritual particle, 7
spiritual potency, 7
state of no-focus, 51
subtle or third eye, 58
subtle power, 16
third eye, subtle, 58
thoughts, 9
trauma, 6
ventilation, 4
Where am I?, 12, 22, 36
withdraw interest, 12

Series

Commentaries

Yoga Sutras of Patanjali

Meditation Expertise

Krishna Cosmic Body

Bhagavad Gita Explained

Anu Gita Explained

Kriya Yoga Bhagavad Gita

Brahma Yoga Bhagavad Gita

Uddhava Gita Explained

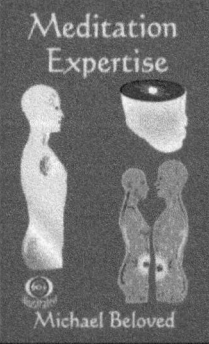

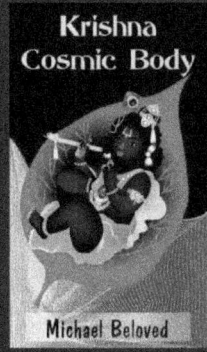 

Yoga Sutras of Patanjali is the globally acclaimed text book of yoga. This has detailed expositions of yoga techniques. Many kriya techniques are vividly described in the commentary.

Meditation Expertise is an analysis and application of the Yoga Sutras. This book is loaded with illustrations and has detailed explanations of secretive advanced meditation techniques which are called kriyas in the Sanskrit language.

Krishna Cosmic Body is a narrative commentary on the Markandeya Samasya portion of the Aranyaka Parva of the Mahabharata. This is the detailed description of the dissolution of the world, as experienced by the great yogin Markandeya who transcended the cosmic deity, Brahma, and reached Brahma's source who is a divine infant Krishna.

Bhagavad Gita Explained shows what was said in the Gita without religious overtones and sectarian biases.

Anu Gita Explained is the detailed description of the effect-energy of current actions in application to future lives.

Kriya Yoga Bhagavad Gita shows the instructions for those who are doing kriya yoga.

Brahma Yoga Bhagavad Gita shows the instructions for those who are doing brahma yoga.

Uddhava Gita Explained shows the instructions to Uddhava which are more advanced than the ones given to Arjuna.

Bhagavad Gita is an instruction for applying the expertise of yoga in the cultural field. This is why the process taught to Arjuna is called karma yoga which means karma + yoga or cultural activities done with a yogic demeanor.

Uddhava Gita is an instruction for apply the expertise of yoga to attaining spiritual status. This is why it is explains jnana yoga and bhakti yoga in detail. Jnana yoga is using mystic skill for knowing the spiritual part of existence. Bhakti yoga is for developing affectionate relationships with divine beings.

Karma yoga is for negotiating the social concerns in the material world and therefore it is inferior to bhakti yoga which concerns negotiating the social concerns in the spiritual world.

This world has a social environment and the spiritual world has one too.

Right now Uddhava Gita is the most advanced informative spiritual book on the planet. There is nothing anywhere which is superior to it or which goes into so much detail as it. It verified that historically Krishna is the most advanced human being to ever have left literary instructions on this planet. Even Patanjali Yoga Sutras which I translated and gave an application for in my book, **Meditation Expertise**, does not go as far as the Uddhava Gita.

Some of the information of these two books is identical but while the Yoga Sutras are concerned with the personal spiritual emancipation (kaivalyam) of the individual spirits, the Uddhava Gita explains that and also explains the situations in the spiritual universes.

Bhagavad Gita is from the *Mahabharata* which is the history of the Pandavas. Arjuna, the student of the Gita, is one of the Pandavas brothers. He was in a social hassle and did not know how to apply yoga expertise to solve it. Krishna gave him a crash-course on the battlefield about that.

Uddhava Gita is from the *Srimad Bhagavatam (Bhagavata Purana),* which is a history of the incarnations of Krishna. Uddhava was a relative of Krishna. He was concerned about the situation of the deaths of many of his relatives but Krishna diverted Uddhava's attention to the practice of yoga for the purpose of successfully migrating to the spiritual environment.

Explained Series

Bhagavad Gita Explained

Anu Gita Explained

Uddhava Gita Explained

The specialty of these books is that they are free of missionary intentions, cult tactics and philosophical distortion. Instead of using these books to add credence to a philosophy, meditation process, belief or plea for followers, I spread the information out so that a reader can look through this literature and freely take or leave anything as desired.

When Krishna stressed himself as God, I stated that. When Krishna laid no claims for supremacy, I showed that. The reader is left to form an independent opinion about the validity of the information and the credibility of Krishna.

There is a difference in the discourse with Arjuna in the Bhagavad Gita and the one with Uddhava in the Uddhava Gita. In fact these two books may appear to contradict each other. In the Bhagavad Gita, Krishna pressured Arjuna to complete social duties. In the Uddhava Gita, Krishna insisted that Uddhava should abandon the same.

The Anu Gita is completely different to the Bhagavad Gita. Krishna refused to display the Universal Form. He quoted a siddha from a higher dimension who lectured on the effect-energies of actions as these construct a person's future opportunities.

Meditation Series

Meditation Pictorial

Meditation Expertise

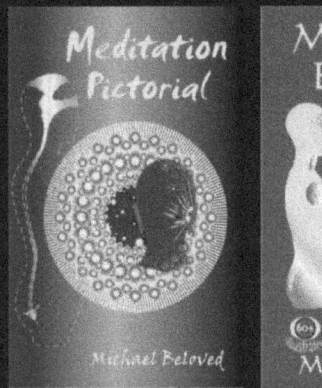

The specialty of these books is the mind diagrams which profusely illustrate what is written. This shows exactly what one has to do mentally to develop and then sustain a meditation practice.

In the **Meditation Pictorial**, one is shown how to develop psychic insight, a feature without which meditation is imagination and visualization, without any mystic experience per se.

In the **Meditation Expertise**, one is shown how to coral one's practice to bring it in line with the classic syllabus of yoga which Patanjali lays out as the ashtanga yoga 8-staged practice.

Both books are profusely illustrated with mind diagrams showing the components of psychic consciousness and the inner design of the subtle body.

Specialty Topics

sex you!

The mystery of sex and reincarnation is explained in detail, not in terms of religion or superstition but by psychic facts which any individual can observe, if he or she can shift focus to the psychic plane. Books like the Bardo Thodol (Tibetan Book of the Dead) and the Egyptian Book of the Dead (Papyrus of Ani), along with Bhagavad Gita, the reincarnation teaching of Buddha and other vital books, took humanity through a spiritual technological leap through time into the hereafter. Perhaps none of these texts dealt with the incidences of sex and reincarnation head on, especially the link between you and the sexual act of your parents which produced your body. In this book you get the details in plain terms without mystery and religious impositions.

Spiritual Master

Practically every positive and negative aspect of having a guru is discussed in this book with recommendations of how to deal with gurus safely. A non-proficient guru can be useful despite his faults, but one must know how to side-step hassles and get to the business at hand, which is to get effective techniques from a spiritual master.

In some cases the spiritual master will be a complete fraud but one should not let that deter one from making spiritual progress in his association. "But why," one might ask, "should one stay with a fraudulent guru?" The answer is that if providence puts one in that position, one should honor providence but one should do so without getting hurt by the unqualified spiritual master. This and similar topics are discussed in this book.

Sleep Paralysis

--- A short to-the-point paper on the psychic cause of sleep paralysis, how to manage it and decrease incidences.

The relationship between sleep paralysis and astral projection is explained. The methods of decreasing the incidences of sleep paralysis, increasing dream recall and being objectively conscious during astral projections is described.

The most revealing part of this paper is the author's description of his sleep paralysis states and what he did to contain these, get out of these and cause his psychic self to separate from and to fuse into the physical body without an incidence.

Astral Projection

--- A paper on reincarnation, subtle body, astral projection, lucid dreaming, sleep paralysis, dimensional hoping, translation to paradise and transit to supernatural places. Astral Projection is a natural psychic function which is not reliant on the conscious awareness of the person concerned. Day after day usually once within every twenty-four hours, an individual spirit is displaced from its physical body but this is usually done while it is in a condition of stupor, where it is not aware that it was separated. It then becomes conscious again as a physical body and gets busy to restart its activities. Astral projection is really the observation of that displaced psyche. Information of how to become conscious of this is divulged in this paper.

English Series

[Bhagavad Gita English](#)

[Anu Gita English](#)

[Markandeya Samasya English](#)

[Yoga Sutras English](#)

[Uddhava Gita English](#)

These are in 21st Century English, very precise and exacting. Many Sanskrit words which were considered untranslatable into a Western language are rendered in precise, expressive and modern English, due to the English language becoming the world's universal means of concept conveyance.

Three of these books are instructions from Krishna. **In Bhagavad Gita English** and **Anu Gita English**, the instructions were for Arjuna. In the **Uddhava Gita English,** it was for Uddhava. Bhagavad Gita and Anu Gita are extracted from the Mahabharata. Uddhava Gita was extracted from the 11th Canto of the Srimad Bhagavatam (Bhagavata Purana). One of these books, the **Markandeya Samasya English** is about Krishna, as described by Yogi Markandeya, who survived the cosmic collapse and reached a divine child in whose transcendental body, the collapsed world was existing. Another of these books, the **Yoga Sutras English,** is the detailed syllabus about yoga practice.

My suggestion is that you read Bhagavad Gita English, the Anu Gita English, the Markandeya Samasya English, the Yoga Sutras English and lastly the Uddhava Gita English, which is much more complicated and detailed.

For each of these books we have at least one commentary, which is published separately. Thus your particular interest can be researched further in the commentaries.

The smallest of these commentaries and perhaps the simplest is the one for the Anu Gita. We published its commentary as the **Anu Gita Explained**. The Bhagavad Gita explanations were published in three distinct targeted commentaries. The first is **Bhagavad Gita Explained**, which sheds lights on how people in the time of Krishna and Arjuna regarded the information and applied it. Bhagavad Gita is an exposition of the application of yoga practice to cultural activities, which is known in the Sanskrit language as karma yoga.

Interestingly, Bhagavad Gita was spoken on a battlefield just before one of the greatest battles in the ancient world. A warrior, Arjuna, lost his wits and had no idea that he could apply his training in yoga to political dealings. Krishna, his charioteer, lectured on the spur of the moment to give Arjuna the skill of using yoga proficiency in cultural dealings including how to deal with corrupt officials on a battlefield.

The second commentary is the **Kriya Yoga Bhagavad Gita**. This clears the air about Krishna's information on the science of kriya yoga, showing that its techniques are clearly described free of charge to anyone who takes the time to read Bhagavad Gita. Kriya yoga concerns the battlefield which is the psyche of the living being. The internal war and the mental and emotional forces which are hostile to self-realization are dealt with in the kriya yoga practice.

The third commentary is the **Brahma Yoga Bhagavad Gita**. This shows what Krishna had to say outright and what he hinted about which concerns the brahma yoga practice, a mystic process for those who mastered kriya yoga.

There is one commentary for the **Markandeya Samasya English**. The title of that publication is **Krishna Cosmic Body**.

There are two commentaries to the Yoga Sutras. One is the **Yoga Sutras of Patanjali** and the other is the **Meditation Expertise**. These give detailed explanations of the process of Yoga.

For the Uddhava Gita, we published the **Uddhava Gita Explained**. This is a large book and requires concentration and study for integration of the information. Of the books which deal with transcendental topics, my opinion is that the discourse between Krishna and Uddhava has the complete information about the realities in existence. This book is the one which removes massive existential ignorance.

Website:

michaelbeloved.com

Forum:

inselfyoga.com

Contact:

axisnexus@gmail.com

Authors

Michael Beloved (Yogi Madhvāchārya) introduced the inSelf Yoga© kundalini and meditation procedure. He first charted the basic mind diagrams and published them in the book *Meditation Pictorial*.

This is for mastery of the 5th stage of yoga, pratyāhāra sensual energy withdrawal, for concentration of soul power and shift of focus to transcendental planes of existence.

Michael designed, used, and tested these methods on the basis of meditation instructions received from several yoga teachers and from the information in the *Bhagavad Gitā*, *Uddhava Gitā*, and *Anu Gitā* and the *Yoga Sūtras of Patanjali*.

devaPriyā Yoginī, who is a certified Sivananda Yoga teacher (2000), is an instructor for the inSelf Yoga© kundalini and meditation procedures. She holds a BA in Psychology from Quincy University and is an active musician, teaching and offering kirtan and forms of spiritual music.

www.ingramcontent.com/pod-product-compliance
Lightning Source LLC
Chambersburg PA
CBHW070629050426
42450CB00011B/3151